Dayslip

Dayship

Helen Lovelock-Burke

MULFRAN PRESS

Published 2011 by Mulfran Press
PO Box 812, Cardiff CF11 1PD
UK
www.mulfran.co.uk

ISBN 1-907327-14-8

Printed by imprint**digital** in Devon [info@imprintdigital.net].

Acknowledgements

Julia Casterton first suggested I put together a collection and had begun to go through my poems when she died. In 2007, Todd Swift took up this task; quite simply, without him this book would not be.

I would like to thank Leona Medlin for deciding to publish *Dayship* and her influence as editor on its final shape. And many thanks are due to Carol Hager who takes what I type on my little Olivetti and makes it look the way I actually want it to look on the page.

A number of these poems were published – some in an earlier version – in the following journals and anthologies: *14, Advance, Assert, Frogmore Papers, Magma, Nthposition, Pause, Poetry Life, and Ver,* and on London and Devon busses. Others were published in connection with the following prizes: The Bridport Prize and Wilkinson Memorial (Birmingham & Midland). 'At the Turn of Sleep' was set to music and performed at the Royal Festival Hall for the Hans Werner Henze festival in March 2001. 'Diane' was projected on a large screen in Trafalgar Square as part of a 2007 promotion of bicycling.

for my children –
Anthony, Thomas,
Francesca & Christopher

Contents

Dayship

A wing of light
makes diamonds on the grass,
a threshold
from which to chart
the history of a day.
Half goes forwards, half
stays in solitude,
a split creed to carry all the hours
firelight on water,
a ship on which to sail.

Fragments

The solid past broke early
when birds came.
It was morning.
I could not fly, be them.
Wisps of sky stay marked
with their sliding shapes.

Puzzled, I collect their shadows,
call out
they are mine and must
be true.

Venetian Vase

Out of sight in a box high up
is a broken vase.
My first lovely thing
bought at a school bazaar
with a dollar my father gave to me
the night I showed that I could read.
I take it out and look at it some time.
Sunlit, its floating colours change:
here Marco Polo's path from China
there the Doge's palace.
Reflected through its frail shape I see
age dark paintings, the battle of Lapanto
and shadowed waterways.

Past days

are close at hand.
They hang with the coats
others with boots in the hall.

Favourites are kept upstairs
in the right hand bureau drawer
with lipsticks, eye pencil and brush.

But some, only for me
are here with old shells
a bottle of scent and my veil.

The Join

I dreamt a party where
I cut my index finger
off: left hand, between
the first and second joint.
It did not matter then
being a dream and meaning something
else. It did not hurt
or bleed. With nine others
I was greedy to want ten.
But then I thought how will I type
f and *r*, *t*, *g*, *b* and *v*?
So I put it in my pocket
where it shrivelled into grey.
Someone, I don't know who,
I knew no one there,
said he knew a great guy
who could fix it up –
or was it she who said – Hurry,
he is a friend of mine,
will do it before he goes to bed.
It was like *Cancer Ward*
but the anaesthetic worked.
When I woke I could not see the join.

Missed

From the door
bright in their orangeness
the kumquats
on the turquoise-green shawl
looked a party.

Obvious leftovers
they still held sunlight,
enough to banish for a moment
the cold northern day.

Beyond them, as if to rest our eyes
almost shining
a pewter dish
was heaped with oyster shells –
they glowed small green sunsets
and I thought
where have I been?
The feast is over. I am too late.

Wedding Dress

Worn first in '29
I was long
in waist, length of arm
sweeping to the floor.

Princess lace
Paris-shaped
so beautiful
people sighed – I
made her fair.

And worn again
three times:
twice my shape held true
to frame their happiness.

Daughter three uplifted
me, changed
to give her waist –
short in front, long in back.

Just yesterday
a daughter's daughter
tried me on –
no one ever thought to check.

Being lace – they'd cut me up
then had to sew
so tight
the threads cannot be found.

The damage done.
I am no longer me.

A Simple Place

Warm on still warm ground
we watched for comets,
traced constellations
and pointed to stars we knew.

We did not mark the air,
dull nightjar's churr
or bend the sounds of grass
but soft in unremembered words
wove that evening high
out of its simple place.

Clouds on the Blackthorn

We curve the land and sky
over this once black
winter thorn and thicket hedge.

Bend into us, bury yourself
in fragile, almost not
scent of dwelling.

Forget summer deep that on green fields rest
forget the solid colour
forget the gift of sloes.

See only us, sun-shaped,
who thought you lived too dark,
came down to rest with you.

In shadow and billowed light
we have made for these few days
the distant earth our home.

Mother's Blouse

It's been years
there in the drawer
always wonder why I keep it
not me at all: grey,
large french tucks from neck to hem
front and back
sleeveless
she had lovely arms –
bought it on their honeymoon
or my father had.

I think I saw her in it once
or maybe it's just –
it is so perfect her.
In my mind she wears it still
floating, silver with auburn hair.

Almost

Outside the window
light changes
as if someone just passed by.

It's always like that
when I think I am alone.
Someone almost comes
to say what I will never hear.

Sometimes I wait at my desk
while sky cradles the day
and silence, which is filled
with the tide of unknown oceans
and the air, with words not said long ago,
breaks as a seventh wave will break
long and wide to foam an empty shore.

Church Bells

Within each hour shapes of time
would lie, stretching, closing up again:
accordions playing high summer sun
to deep north-eastern storms.

Each hour rang its cadence:
a boy's call muffled in the mist
as dawn fog lifted
to show bare feet and a jumping dog.

On those days the foghorn would warn
late into the morning
overriding gulls circling inland,
till at last a whippoorwill would call

to sun or storm or rain
where minutes grew so out of shape
seconds could not hold
to sixty beats of time.

On a 747

I remember
when I was young
and flew with you.
Air whispered the canopy
propeller blurred
as we curved above the land
we knew, small,
free in a wider sky.

As I watch the cloud,
column, heap and dome,
press down the earth
somewhere there
below
as we incline through the sky
I remember us.
We flew.

Northern Lights

New England, 1946

Cold filled our eyes,
covered us,
coats and flap-eared hats,
slipped into our boots
and on to the frosted grass.

We were strange from our deep-sleep waking
excited by his sudden command:
"come children, quick
out, under the sky".
We watched
silent as the stillness around us.

Through iridescent starring of air
miles of gossamer scarf
rippled and floated
fluting the sun born wind.
Shadowed in greens it crested the sky
skirted the whisper of earth.

Something More

Telephone poles hang wire on the air
for something more than talk, see how the young
tight-gripping swallows hold at training time,

hear how the wind makes a gift to us
then listen as the different sounds are sung, when
telephone poles hang wire on the air.

There, beyond the barn in the old meadow
the wire strands its way across for young
tight-gripping swallows at their training time.

To the east by the road just after dawn
the sun will send a silver shiver through
telephone poles, that hang wire on air

to thread the morning light with open day.
In that rush and skelter hour workers wake,
go to their jobs, tight-gripped at training time.

They use the phone and forget in stuffy
rooms, telephone poles and all that happens
when they hang their wire on the air
for young tight-gripping swallows at training time.

"Follow"

It was a game we played, have you forgotten
how it grew within us
how we were silent in the shadows
waiting to take our chance
how we climbed the trees
to see and not be seen
how quiet, through the crisp of leaves
we followed, slow or fast
each one apart?

Have you forgotten all the rules:
how, always free to go,
we knew how long to stay?
Do you remember how we followed
just to change the way we went
never saying why?

Remember, you must remember
how words were never used.
It was as if when we were out
from under the trees
out of their shadows
we would find the night too big
for words, and how after
even in our sleeping
we could never speak
of the stillness we had heard.

Amiens

It was one of those chances
claimed as a miracle then
that up through dust of the broken town
high on its hill of steps
above skirts of coloured, shattered glass
the cathedral shell survived.

On our Sunday
there were rainbows on washed cobbles
and fresh bread in the early morning air.
At the top of the steps the vibrato of bells
closed our eyes. The new-made town receded.

From the entrance
we could see up the long nave
to the cross over the main altar
where those who knelt
were blurred by morning
that poured in great fans
through clear glass in tall Gothic windows.

Frost on the Ground

When the purple turns dark
you will close the curtains.
There was frost on the ground last night.

In this day just past
a day in which I lived
you were away.

You did not see
lapwings dance the field
one last time, or hear

by the back door
sparrows crowd the hedge.
But most of all you missed

the white smell of snowdrop
new grass and tight furled green.
I had those things.

A Silver Sea

Day had waited in time that did not move.
All day the still sun burned from a flat sky

while air scratched hard drawn breath
heavy, in lost single shapes of light.

Colourless, in hot haze it waited
for afternoon to move and gentle earth.

Now in sudden softness all blades of green
single, gold-rimmed, turn, then move as one

in a changed quiet touching through the corn –
a wave unbreaking in a silver sea.

Sisters

In a sharp of light –
the mirror we shared
each thinking only the other was fair
dressing together then talking late
our toes curled into our hands.

Why think of that now
or how playing in the surf
you lost two teeth
and the times you sneaked
when I didn't wear shoes?

Days, "safe" and long ago,
over coffee we'd talk of those things,
the news, our children,
never the years between.

The Night Waders

Our few words fade.
Stars silver us
in the silence,
as we sit watching

our children glimmering
in phosphorescent shallows
star-dipping to gather monad,
hand, calf, part-lit face

reflected, shining,
on starred-dark water.

Clocks

In that first moment, just then
when waking is
and hours lie about full and fat,
ready to feed plans that wait to be a past
of things that have been done

even then as sun strides the window
and floods a daylight
too bright to have shape –
even as the seconds open
minutes start to count
get thin and tight so they can fold
tidy, into clocks.

It's Not As If

It's not as if the moon and tides are still
or oceans and seas are flat, but softly
as morning ends the dawn, we grow away.

Above childhood days and wide, star filled nights
we were sure, that there, a vivid heaven lay.
It's not as if the moon and tides are still

or currents of air banished the flight of birds
but slowly, as age encircles us,
and morning ends the dawn, we turn away.

Do you remember how on the bomb sites
light blazed the shattered glass and daisies grew?
It's not as if the moon and tides are still

but rushed, our eyes forget. In crowded rooms
with busy sounds we work toward success
and in the noise we make, we fade away.

Our search for all the things we think we're owed
has stilled our wonder and our questioning.
It's not as if the moon and tides are still –
but morning ends the dawn. We grow away.

First Movie

What could a movie be
to keep us, a line, waiting,
hot instead of by the sea?

Redbrick sidewalk, clapboard houses
horse chestnut trees and us
simmered under a late August sky.

Standing in shade I watched sun
spark windows opposite
in Mr Allen's dry goods store,

saw small puffs of cloud,
free. But I was down in the rows
of us on Main Street.

We wiggled in summer best
humming out our noise. Parents
were few, looked tall, stood still.

The sun almost down when we came out
dazed, imperfectly ourselves
blinking in brightness.

Bricks still hot as slanting rays
brought sunset and ocean change.
Touched, leaves lifted in the clean cool

of early evening. Day slid into opal
while parents stood and talked,
and children fooled around.

I drifted into quiet, saw the town wharf
dark on reflecting water, the harbour
lights just reaching out,

smelled seaweed on the air
sharp with tide turn, heard gulls
and the clinking of stays.

Landward, as we walked home
stars began to show. The still heat-ended
night breathed wild honeysuckle.

A Kind of Silence

The words she did not say
words to kindle and to share
to make life light
were words we did not know.

One cold clear New York day
walking home I saw her
across on the other side
in sunlight
with people I did not know.

Through noise and flow of traffic
in broken bits I watched
how standing still
she skipped and ran with light
and laughter as she talked.

That day, seeing her sparkling so,
I knew why people thought
her wonderful, knew too
how childhood might have been.

My Father's House

On that last day
he took me with him when he walked
to the harbour light. We stood for a while
looking out toward Cape Poge, clear after storm
and watched the whitecaps coming in,
cut as if with pinking shears,
against a fall blue sky.

You ask about my father's house.
What do you ask?
The city building where we went to live
or there where I can see us,
our backs to me
bright in the after-storm
circled in sun-caught spray?

I reach through the years
touch my learning
with his voice in my head
as natural and as neutral as the wind.

The Floors Were Painted Each Spring

The floors were painted each spring
not bright or dark
but a blue that children like, call blue.

The first thing we did
was help drag the mattresses outside
or if it was raining
put them up against the wall in the kitchen behind the Franklin Stove
under the hot water tank.
Rain meant we slept on blankets
till the weather turned.

Then we would wash down the house
to get rid of mould and damp –
but always right through the summer
when we pressed down in sleep
the smell of old salt damp was there like happiness.

We always brought too many clothes –
maybe it was to fill up the blanket trunks
or to make us feel important – or maybe there was hope each year
we would be tidy summer children.

The same shorts and tops, a parka, heavy sweater
and one pair of jeans for protection
from poison ivy when we went through the Indian woods.
We didn't have a clothes washer, so we tied our tops
through the arms, and jeans and shorts through belt holes
to drag them after us as we sailed to Cape Poge and back.

Later when we were older, wore more clothes and cared a bit
someone opened a launderette in town
but still we did the jeans the old way.

We never used shoes,
just sneakers for blackberrying
or when we saw our mother in the town marketing
we'd stop our bicycles and put them on to make her happy.

High in the Oak

The sound of leaves touching
tells if the weather will change.
Shadows on the uneven platform
reflect green, stain my skin.

As I climbed up
the rope ladder swung out and back
against the ridged deep bark.

Now the sweet smell of old wood on which I lie
and the sharp, snapping smell of living oak
as it reaches up and around me
layer the air.

Here, high and away, here
in this tree place we made –
my sons and I – I come, now they are grown.

Soon I will get up, lean out
on and across young branches,
float as I bend with them
swaying with the sky over light-filled land.

Unheard Sound

Going around my life each day
I touch those words
to the four of you
I did not stop to say.
They spring at the oddest times:
rising steam, from a new poured cup of tea
will pause to draw a face
or weeding in the garden
one of you will echo from a tree
another almost touch my cheek
in the empty house I will clearly hear
my youngest not rushing down the stair.

Unheard they keep company
in words there is no need to say.

Lost

Sometimes things get lost
not just for a while
but absolutely:

eyeglasses
my pen, full of words
the book not yet in my mind
that poem I used to know by heart
a photograph no one else remembers
put down in its everyday
or safely
in a safe place
now, not there
or anywhere any more.

They are away
the ready and the almost ready:
a letter, just one word to add
the box kept for overseas at Christmas time.
They are not.

But time, when lost
is unbegotten
never there to have had
to keep, as memory.

At least lost things
were here, were touched.

Split Time

Today had two parts

> the bedroom when I woke
> stairs as I went up and down
> a dog walk in the rain
> the boiler room where I hung the wash to dry

my hands did all the things my hands have learnt to do
vegetables, tidying, ironing and sorting out the fridge

but all the time

> a misted lake, listening deer
> and mountains in lapis shadows,
> lived in music
> invested long ago

a swan danced within me
a painter shaped the light.

Cathedrals

On land near here
is a small rise, an undulation
that would fall away unnoticed
except for trees that stand
in congregation
to an unremembered time.
Birds canopy in crowded song.
Untarnished
the sun slants patterns
worked in stone.

Flying Dream

A stranger stood by the icebox.
He smiled
then we danced.
He was shorter –

but such fun.
We didn't speak, but dreamwise
he asked to marry.
I said "Yes"!

The ring was over
the other side of the room
and happy, loving him so – to be quick
I flew.

It was just a little flight
I thought no one would notice
but they did and right away
started gossiping.

I walked back, weaving in and out of all the people
hoping he would not mind.
But he did.
So we called it off.

Reaching for Cranberry Sauce

It must have been the cold
coming up from the freezer –
or maybe my hand, bright lit
by display lights
as I reached across the frozen food
that took me back:

there was an ancient feel
where thick green moss,
which covered the boulders
on their sunless side,
paled on east and west
round to good grey granite.

We would climb up
on late fall days
when it was too cold to swim
too rough to sail
and scrape the moss away.
We always hoped to find runes
the Norsemen left.

Cranberries were hectic in the bogs below.
We would pick them for their brightness
wonder who first cracked them with their teeth
and did not die.

The Last Time I Saw Paris

And there by Green Park
I'm in Paris again
young, with friends –
dreamlike, but

it breathes into now
bringing with it
croissant, the smell of coffee
and talk of what to do.

Sparrows made more sense, –
gathered crumbs, flew, settled,
flew again in their scherzo
of birdcall and wing-shift,

a prelude to days
that held the light
of Renoir, Sisley and Monet
in city and river valley.

The leaves were pale
just opened with lemon silhouettes.
Girls wore skirts, walked
dancing their reality.

Single patrons lifted their heads
as they passed,
forgot coffee and papers, adrift
in the music of the morning.

The Time Before

Remember the time before
when she did not know
what it was to wish?

Wish was a non-word
like *the* or *black*.
The did not need
to be
not saying anything
it was nothing.
And *black*
even on the darkest night
sky glimmered earth,
even in a closet once
there were sparks
inside
her head,
which she tried to tell.

Wish was sound
of swimming and the sea.
It was the saddest word
she learnt to know
needing it one day.

In Wrinkled Light

The apple tree
bends over the roof
toward me as I stand
on the edge of the bath

to see the town clock
just dawn, clear
and no wind yet. Climb down
in sweater, shorts and top

to bicycle with my brother
through the mauve morning,
ready our boat
and wait, sails unfurled

in the stillness
for the first ripples
on the flat
reflecting bay.

There is no one,
even the fishermen sleep.
Just us at sunrise, sailing
on Sundays, before Mass.

Your Stop

It was you who said that we should stop.
It was odd
to stop
if we were just
to start
once more.
Why did we not
go on –
be as we were?

Now some days
I see the place you made us stop
that desert
while you made up your mind
and how in that long wait
I finally turned away
saw a blade of grass
arch to silver
and the sky gathering for night.

Nursery Rhyme

This is the way we live our life
inside myself
I, from a distance, sing.

As the words go round
and come again, they touch
in my caught breath

a church fair, and fields
bright with goldenrod
when childhood sang

This is the way to pass
goodbyes once said.
I never knew the strength each held.

Unseen children sing
a discarded self.

Diane

I always meant to ask
whose bike it was you used.
No one didn't have one –
though you were extra –
that last summer there.

We went barefoot –
you wore sneakers all the time.
That was the summer
we discovered boys, or they discovered us.
I wonder how it would have been
if you hadn't come?

Would I have stayed the same
never square-danced
in swirling fifties skirts – caring
to put lipstick on
and brush my hair so it was smooth on top
like yours?

Would I have cinched my waist
stood sideways to the mirror
to see what shape I had
or thought of heels?
My brother's friends fell for you
then saw me too.

There's a picture he took of us
walking away through mist
me ankle deep in foam
you higher up the slant of beach.
You have a hat on, we hold hands.

Patience

It is afternoon.
Along the street
women fold into their cars.
Parcels bend them,
children pull them,
this hot day.

In a tight old Morris
a mother sits
hand on wheel, head down
holding time
heavy with the thought
of calm.

Worry

It is the matter of feet
that I worry about:

if they could just behave
I would not wish for wings.

Mine are so heavy
there at the end of my legs.

They should dance and leap
when I feel like this

forward foot gliding
over the air, trailing
the other behind.

Please Give Me

Please: red satin shoes
that call the poppies from my dress
please – diamond buckles
and music and lines of candlelight
that swing the room with me and yes
of course, the you of yesterday, held close
to spin and dance the steps away,
away the years and years, the stiffness in my limbs.
Safe again I'll close my eyes
catch the flying past.

Standing

in the wind my hair
rides out from me. Landlocked I
taste a storm at sea.

Early Morning Snow

Snow is a music
on trees and lane
but we are too old.

How will we get to town?
How is it out on the road?
Questions overfill the whiteness.

Evening Barbecue

Nutted coals shift,
pale, the fire spent.
On the long lie of land
far trees etch their shape.

The young are quiet
silhouettes,
on the afterglow.
Some talk, some still eat

unaware.
One stands as if to go.
Stops, sees.
Is still.

Safe

A sort of death follows time across the room
to listen to the space between
two ticks of the ticking clock
to the deftly balanced minute
as it waits between the three and four
as if to give a chance
not speak, until, with an almost thud
a tiny, tidy second lives, moves on.

The room has shape again
and time is back in place.
The unsaid is safe once more
and cannot add
another end to ends of long ago.

Unseen

Naked, alone
to run and swim
with nothing on
to feel the water
touching
in forgiveness of my age
caressing
in some wonder
of remembered youth
to spring out,
Aphrodite,
wet to the sun
light on eyelashed rainbows
on drops and fine arm-hairs
that flood and steam
my half-seen curves
feel warmth
on me turn hot.

Requiem

You go each day
a little further,
shrouded
in the present.
We both know
you are going.
Not now, but soon.
Let's pretend
the lock is jammed.
Leave today outside.

It is easier that way
to stay in the fortress
where summer does not move
and the corn stays green.
It is wiser not to be sure
what time light says it is.

A Photograph

You are still and silent.
Stopped there. That moment, past.
Stopped as in some blind and sudden falling.
Stopped as in that is all.

As if the Niagara
could stop there at the Falls,
the St. Lawrence not be.
As if in the years that come
just this in my hand.

As if death could hold
the basin
and the gorge
the haze of rainbow
that touched and coloured
full flowing to the open sea.

Without a Camera

One is of two boys,
you can tell by the cut of their hair.
They are small
the tadpole age
when seeing is to touch, eat or climb.
The bridge is stone
their shoulders' height.
On tip-toe
they have just thrown sticks –
one's arm is out of focus –
they are looking down, watching.
A rose, a buddleia
one pink, one violet, untended for years
spray a wild, wide fan behind them.

The other is of us two
walking down a hill.
We are close, but not touching.
The setting sun sends slow shadows
across cobbles
curving each on each to the other side
where sun-shapes mark
shops, open door fronts, tables.
People sit, stand, quiet or talking.
Pots, waiting to be bought, line both sides.
Halfway down bougainvillea scarlets a wall.
We are walking into the evening
where fields, long stone walls
and poplar trees shape the land.

At the Turn of Sleep

To bring
to bring at waking
from the shadows of the mind
as at the turn of year

to bring
out of deep some completely unknown loss
that rests in the moment as at the turn of sleep

to bring
forth – from under the rhythm of an ordinary life
in that waking moment – what was lost

to bring
in that brief gift the why
why, why the sense of loss
that shadows in the sunlight of the mind.

Visitor

He's here again,
his shadow nearly fell.

Sometimes,
at least from the kitchen window,
I almost see the morello cherry of his coat
his moleskin trousers, soft boots.

He moves quickly, but still
fatigue rides him and his spattered clothes.

His horse?
In a stable backing on the barn
or there, blowing hard
the other side of now.

Tomorrow

There was always tomorrow
to plan, then go – touch
the sky on a high mountain pass
where Alexander marched.

The Parthenon waited,
olive groves on Mount Olympus,
and Delphi in the cool smell of pine.

I would see the pyramids,
Abu Simbel,
the sand thirsting for moonlight.

Somehow waiting for tomorrow
I gathered how to be:
saw the spring grass grow

heard summer sound
fold into night
as tide slipped sea away.

In the slowing down to autumn
in the clear cold smell of winter
I've heard the curlew call

and stretched my arms
to cup the bowl of sky
as, clear of cloud,
it shaped our evening light.

Part of Day

This
the part of day
that is practice
for death.

It has power only to rest
as light rests
when duty ties it down
to wait for night.

In this hour words
from forgotten prayer
echo the unrecorded shapes
that formed in the silences
of childhood.

In Return

A strange story
maybe I could give you that
as it is too late for love.

So here we are, a stone woman,
a bit of granite,
with a wind-blown skirt
and you way off there.

If I give, will you
deed the wind to me
smelling of home?

Holborn Tube

I should have stopped
there at the top of Holborn tube
written down the words
that overflowed the moving stair –
there, before going through the gate
stooped to catch them
as they fell from me
rolled back down
or slid forward
underneath

in that scary flat-stair way.
Now each time I pass my ticket through the slot
new ghosts will worry me
uncaught words will scorn
each time my love be lost again
as I exit here at Holborn.

The Watcher

Something is on the farm track
there under that tree,
indefinite, through low sun.

It is there yet does not move.
Its shadow lies in the field, long,
balanced as if it too is waiting.

Will it still be there,
man-shaped, in the morning

or will the warm sound of bumble bees
with early summer shining
on their black and gold

be so real the watcher will forget
and the one who waits under the tree
like a question never asked.

By the Window

Here by the window
unheeded days layer the past
sunlight fills the place where shadows ran
and voices used to call.

Here is beyond this place and its view:
forsythia mingles with the thorn.

Beyond the this-I-see
rest all the hours
when cowslips glowed
white in the moonlight.

Bring to me

a fan of light
and one long shadow
melting in the evening grass,

that poem
by the open door
as it rested there waiting to be

and the taste
of spring that floats forever
in still April air. Simplest of all

bring me the space
between tulips as they reach
and bend in mirrors reflecting them.

Breathless

You and your cousin, each day more real
both waited for with joy.

Your newness curved your mother's time
two months behind your cousin's as she grew;

laughter was so easy and every day
sun, rain or wind held light.

As sometimes happens
breathless on a heavy August day

I held the phone, said I know not what
just not to cry against your mother's pain.

In your cousin's smile and in her reaching out
I have a trace of you.

Sail

When small-boat-sails shape the sky
when I hear a voice skipping
as sea skips the wind
the day I am in gybes
changes tack and I am again
with you or you with me
sailing as we used to
reading windscapes
one to the other.

The Morning

No one told me of the morning
that it had another self.
No one told how it sang
without a need for sound.

No one told of stillness
as it waited for the dawn,
never how light was held
before the sun was up

never of unseen hills,
the shape their shadows cast
of meadows, of colour and of air
before we start to speak.

No one told me blades of grass
could safely fence a dream.